UNCOVERING THEOLOGIES in Genesis

An Interactive Exploration of the Deep Structures of Interpretation

UNCOVERING THEOLOGIES in Genesis

An Interactive Exploration of the Deep Structures of Interpretation

Genevive Dibley, PhD

GlossaHouse
Uncovering Theologies Series

Uncovering Theologies in Genesis:

An Exploration of the Deep Structures of Interpretation
© 2019 by GlossaHouse

Dibley, Genevive, 1974 -
Uncovering Theologies in Genesis: An Exploration of the Deep Structures of Interpretation / Genevive Dibley. GlossaHouse, 110 Callis Circle, Wilmore, KY 40390
x, 99 ; 25.4 cm.
ISBN: 978-1942697923 (paperback)
Library of Congress Control Number:

1. Bible. Genesis--Illustration. 2. Bible. Genesis--Interpretation. 3. Bible. Theology. Genesis. 4. Bible. Genesis--Textbooks. I. Title. II. Dibley, Genevive
Book and Cover Design by Genevive Dibley and Jason Marshall

for my daughters

Langsea and Lucy

who I fervently wish would
not grow up

and for my *Dad*
who taught me how to draw

ACKNOWLEDGEMENTS

This project is deeply indebted to Jason Marshall who defines the concept of a good friend. A novice to this kind of project, I had no idea what I was asking when I solicited his help in laying out this book. At every turn Jason – an artist and designer – has made this project better. He has been an encouraging and patient teacher and generous beyond measure with his time and talent.

Eternal thanks to my daughters (10 and 11 years old) who were righteously offended on my behalf when my editor, Fred Long, reflected in an early discussion that my drawings were perfect for this project because they were "not too good" and so would not intimidate students attempting to draw alongside them. While he has tried to take it back – my little avenging angels are slow to forgive his slight. They also contributed their own artwork to this book (cover art of Eve thinking by Langsea, and the three thinking people on page xvi by Lucy).

His opinion of my drawings aside, I am nonetheless grateful to Fred who had the editorial imagination capable of envisioning the value and feasibility of this project. He has been encouraging at every turn allowing me the freedom and the time to bring my vision of this project into being.

I am grateful to my friend Cherice Ullrich, a middle and high school religion teacher at Rockford Christian School, who experimented with the Uncovering Theologies project in her classes and whose feedback was instrumental in developing the introductory material.

I must acknowledge the long suffering Rockford University students on whom I experimented endlessly in creating the Uncovering Theologies project. Reading and analyzing their interpretations of the Bible with them has been both a delight and a revelation.

Last but certainly not least, I owe much thanks to my husband Peter. Without his unfailing support and material assistance in domestic matters, our children would have been eating cereal for dinner most nights as I try to finish my various projects.

CONTENTS

General introduction   Page xiii

Student introduction   Page xiv

FAQ   Page xviii

Instructor introduction   Page xix

Adam and Eve - Genesis 3:1-24   Page 1

Cain and Able - Genesis 4:1-16   Page 33

Sacrifice of Isaac - Genesis 22:1-14   Page 61

UNCOVERING THEOLOGIES in Genesis

An Interactive Exploration of the Deep Structures of Interpretation

General Introduction

Authors cannot write everything. They make choices as to what lines of the narrative to sketch into place, which aspects of the narrative demand more detail, and what they can leave in the unarticulated shadows. The choices an author feels at liberty to make has everything to do with how much common ground the author believes they share with their readers (their intended audience). The greater the points of continuity imagined – language, culture, history, worldview, mythology, experience, theology, etc. – the more the author can afford to signal or shorthand or leave unexplained elements of the narrative resting in the assumption that the intended audience will understand intuitively how to fill these "gaps" in the narrative.

Why is this the case? To hold a narrative thread, to create drama, to build emotion, to keep the attention of the reader, an author cannot explain every element in the story and hold the narrative together. For example, if a modern author wanted to tell a story about the anger of a teenager wanting to attend a party but denied access to the family car – the tension of the moment, any dialogue the author might want to write, would suffer greatly if before they could write the next sentence the author first had to stop and dedicate a long paragraph explaining what a car is and then another to explain what a party is. The narrative would be terribly long and disjointed.

It falls, then, to the reader to fill the gaps in a narrative. Readers supply missing detail, decide the implication of textual signals, assume a structural matrix for the narrative drawn from their own knowledge and experience. Often this narrative gap filling – the thousands of assumptions made in the course of reading – happens just below the conscious awareness of the reader. So while the author intends their text to mean something (likely specific), the reader plays an active role in what a text can mean to them. This thing readers do in filling the narrative gaps is the act of interpretation.

Have you ever wondered why people read the same text and have such different interpretations?

The level of continuity between an author and a reader is assumed necessarily in the mind of the author. However, once written and released into the world, an author loses control of who reads their work and when it is read. Each successive reader receiving the text must draw from their own deep structure in turn to fill the narrative gaps to make sense and meaning of the text. The farther in time and culture a reader stands from the time and culture of the authors, the greater the margin for interpretive variation. This is how people reading biblical texts can look at the same passage and sincerely come away with very different interpretations.

It is often the case however that readers think of themselves as passive recipients of an author's ideas. They do not tend to think they are interpreting, do not realize the degree to which they are making all manner of micro-interpretive assumptions, but rather assume that they are reading the plain sense of a passage. Understanding the act of reading as a necessarily interpretive exercise is one of the critical first steps in responsible biblical interpretation. What is it you bring to the text? What assumptions are you making? Where does your deep structure – your society, your values, your theology, the cultural debates of your time – get superimposed on to the biblical text? Before you can begin to understand what a biblical author was intending to say in a given passage (let alone how later authors interpreted the passage relative to their time and place) you must grasp the nature of narrative and interpretation. The Uncovering Theologies project is a creative exploration of that interpretive process.

How to use Uncovering Theologies

What you get:

There are three stories from the Hebrew Bible: Adam and Eve, Cain and Abel, and the Sacrifice of Isaac (the Akeda). Each story is represented in its entirety. The text is in the New Revised Standard English translation. Each section of text has an accompanying illustration. The narrative has been overtly "gapped" meaning blank panels have been spliced into the narrative.

What you do:

Your job is to pull the narrative through the blank panels. Draw a scene that links the panels proceeding and following. Then compose two or three lines of text narrating your panel on the lines provided below.

AND THE POINT OF THIS IS…?

Imagine the elements of the story as the bricks. An author arranges the bricks in a pattern constructing the edifice of the narrative. The author might stack the bricks loosely or tightly together – either way there are inevitably spaces between the bricks. A reader's mind, making sense of the story, will reflexively fill those gaps with a kind of interpretive mortar which cements the structure together in the mind of the reader. The composition of the mortar will vary from reader to reader as it is drawn from the reader's context.

Now imagine that once the reader has read the story and understood it, we could pull the bricks, the author's story elements, out of the wall leaving just the mortar. What comprised the reader's interpretation would be revealed and could be examined in its own right. This is what the Uncovering Theologies project does. This exercise will reveal to you, perhaps for the first time, what exactly your interpretive mortar is composed of. Many people who endeavor to read the Bible do not realize the level to which they are interpreting the text. It is often surprising to them to discover where they draw from to fill a gap in the narrative. It can be another biblical story, another biblical book, a teaching from their youth, a song, a movie, or something else entirely.

HOW TO THINK ABOUT IT

Step 1:   First read the story again familiarizing yourself with the arc of the narrative and the details.

Step 2:   Look through the illustrations noting where they are divided.

Step 3:   Get up and get a cup of coffee or tea or hot chocolate and let your mind wander over the project for a couple of minutes, see what surfaces. What do you imagine motivates the characters of the narrative to make the choices they do (don't forget God is a character in these stories as well)? What do you imagine was the backstory to this tale? What details do you wonder about? What doesn't make sense?

Step 4:   Don't panic. Students (because they believe they are reading the plain sense of the passage) often think they have nothing to say or are afraid of making a mistake. There are literally no wrong ways to link the panels – THERE ARE NO WRONG ANSWERS!

Step 5:   Don't over think it. Draw simply and quickly. Your drawing skill does not factor. Write what comes to mind in the first five minutes and then move on. If you would like to draw more – finish the entire story and go back and en-hance your illustrations.

Step 6:   Have fun!

Lucy! 10

AND THE VALUE OF THIS IS...?

An appreciation of the narrative "gaps" in biblical narrative can foster:

1: **The invitation** - the Uncovering Theologies Project creates an appreciation for how biblical texts invite the reader to interpret and so make the text mean something to them in their social-historical context.

2: **The revelation** - the Uncovering Theologies project surfaces the reader's latent, reflexive interpretation, a thing often hidden or unknown to the reader as they believe themselves to be reading the plain meaning of the text.

3: **The analysis** - the Uncovering Theologies project makes the reader's interpretation visible allowing them to recognize their interpretive tendencies, to identify the texts, traditions, and teachings they leveraged to make sense of the biblical story.

4: **The evolution** - the Uncovering Theologies project cultivates an understanding of how interpretations of texts evolve over centuries within traditions in realizing that ancient interpreters – the later biblical authors, the Rabbis, Church Fathers, and Imams – were equally bound by their own cultural context in interpreting biblical texts.

5: **The charity** - the Uncovering Theologies project enhances the reader's ability to appreciate the interpretations of other readers even when there is interpretive disagreement. It fosters the recognition that all reader's interpretive "mortar" with which they fill the narrative "gaps" is drawn from a particular social-historical locality.

6: **The danger** - the Uncovering Theologies project exposes maladapted interpretive impulses allowing the student to recognize bigoted, prejudicial, anti-Semitic or misogynist strains in interpretations and (with compassionate guidance) begin to wrestle with identifying what motivates dangerous interpretations in themselves and others.

A reductive introduction Jewish midrash

Midrash is an ancient technique/methodology/style/approach/orientation to reading sacred Jewish literature which sought, and still seeks, to plumb the depths of the interpretative potential of a given text. At the center of midrashic endeavors is the presupposition that scared literature is multivalent. Those engaging in midrashic readings look beyond the literal, face value meanings of a pericope in favor of reading into, through, and behind text paying attention to the words and the sounds of words drawing connections to other texts which may not seem at first to relate. Ancient religious theorists and the rabbis (teachers) were particularly adept at identifying gaps in the text, things not explained, which invited interrogation and inter-pretation. The second century C.E. collections of the rabbi's interpretations, insight, and teachings are known as the tannaitic midrashim.

FAQ:

1.	**Do I have to draw?**	YES! Drawing accesses other parts of your brain and can bring things you did not know you thought to light because you are picturing the scene.
2.	**Do I have to write an explanation?**	YES! While you know what you mean to depict with your illustration, it will likely be less clear to everyone else. Write a few lines explaining what is happening or voicing the characters internal monologue. Perhaps you imagine they might have said more things to each other than the biblical author recounts. If you have a lot more to say, use the additional lines on the back of the panel.
3.	**I can only draw stick people...**	Perfect. No more is needed.
4.	**I can't think of anything to say...**	No problem. There is a menu of prompts to help you if you get stuck. Use a prompt like: therefore... so that... in order to... however... and then... Think about entering into the story from the perspective of one of the characters – what would they make of what is happening? Alternatively, it may be helpful to imagine yourself explaining this story to someone else, perhaps a child or a challenging adult interlocutor. What question might they ask of the story at the points it is gapped? How would you respond to make sense of the tale?
5.	**I need more space! I have more to say in a certain gap.**	No problem. Split the blank panel in half and draw two scenes.
6.	**I don't like how the drawing/s are done. I would have drawn the scene differently.**	Fantastic. Change it. Draw it better on a separate paper and paste it over the existing illustration.
7.	**I think a gap/s is in the wrong place.**	Fair. A little trickier to alter but change it! Or make a note of where the gap should go – your professor will find it very interesting.
8.	**There should be a gap but there isn't.**	Excellent! Add the panel/s you need. Cut, paste, redraw as you need to.
9.	**I don't like the NRSV translation at some point/s.**	Outstanding. Fix it. If you read Hebrew, offer your own translation. If you prefer another translation of the Bible other than the NRSV at a certain point, substitute it and then take the time to explain why you prefer the other translation.

Instructor introduction

One of the critical challenges in teaching biblical and Pseudepigraphical literature is how to help students become aware of their own interpretive biases. Often such self-awareness is difficult to achieve as students raised in biblically based religious traditions feel themselves to be thoroughly familiar with the text as they have heard countless sermons and teachings on the Bible. They are further, unwittingly hamstrung in literary-critical studies by inherited systems of theology causing them to alternately read into passages what is not there, anticipate and insert the arguments of much later authors or miss altogether critical interpretive details of a passage. On this account, such students have little inherent ability to appreciate the interpretive, midrashic genius of the post-prophetic writers and early Jewish apocalypticists of the Second Temple period who so adroitly exploited the textual gaps left by earlier biblical authors. Slow to grasp the methodologies and strategies of these authors, they miss the significance of their import for the composition and reception of the New Testament and Qur'an.

In an attempt to speed the process of self-discovery, I have experimented with having students compose graphic novels on pivotal biblical passages drawn from Israel's mythic tales of origin (Garden of Eden, the Akedah, etc.). Students are given a narrative pericope in which the scenes of the biblical tale appear illustrated in frames (as in a comic book). Each illustrated frame is followed by a blank frame which students are asked to fill (illustrate and provide text) using prompts like "therefore", "on account", or "so that". The narrative mortar the students supply in linking the elements of the tale surfaces their own midrashic interpretations resulting in a much deeper engagement with the text far earlier in the course and a more profound appreciation of the ancient authors' contribution to the tradition.

As a professor, the Uncovering Theologies project gave me an unprecedented window into the theologies of my students. The novels allowed me to know with some precision the students' orientations which, in turn, enabled me to better identify the driving concerns and interests behind their questions. Many of the discussions we had in class were raw and honest, at times confessional. One, for example, regarding the punishment of Eve evolved into a discussion about the nature of power between men and women and whether consensual sex is a fiction men allow women in the modern world. This then led to a candid discussion about sexual assault on campus. During another discussion concerning the sacrifice of Isaac, a young woman revealed she had given up a baby for adoption in her teens and likened the social and familial pressure to do so as a sacrifice. It was a deeply moving, compassionate reading in which she challenged her peers not only in their interpretation of Abraham within the narrative but how these narratives speak to and into the lives of modern readers.

Scalability of the project: Whether you teach graduate school or elementary school, the Uncovering Theologies project invites students of any level to discover themselves as interpreters.

Elementary level: Drawing unlocks children's imaginations. The invitation to draw within the biblical story beckons children to have ideas about what they are reading. A teacher might opt to have students draw independently and then bring the class together to share and compare their ideas or project the image and work as a class/group together to discuss how to fill the gap.

Junior high level: The stories in the Uncovering Theologies project are well known stories for any junior high age student growing up in the synagogue, church or mosque. The familiarity of the tales causes students to assume that they have read and understood the stories. Often, however, the student has been told these stories, taught them with an accompanying interpretation by a parent or Sunday school teacher or movie, and have never really read the stories for themselves. The Uncovering Theologies project forces a junior high age student to slow down and think through a text. In a classroom/youth group setting, a teacher or group leader can invite students to share their work and discuss the implications. It is fascinating what they will contribute.

High school level: Through the exercises of the Uncovering Theologies project students at the high school level to come to understand how biblical texts invite interpretation. Students discover themselves to be not merely readers but interpreters. With an instructor's help, either individually or collectively in a classroom setting, students can come to understand which sources (textual, cultural, etc.) they are bringing into conversation with the biblical story they are working with. For example, students will read aspects of the book of Job into Genesis 3 inventing a backstory for the serpent. The disclosure of these kinds of syntheses ("mashups" make an effective music analogy) are nearly always a revelation to the student. The effect is not significantly lessened if the instructor only has time to discuss a few examples in class. There is a place for instructor notes on the back of the students' panels. With guidance, a student's discovery of themselves as an interpreter can be parlayed into an understanding of others, even those who hold different interpretations of the same passage, as interpreters equally. The experience of charitably listening to others explain how they understand a passage opens avenues beyond whether an interpretation is right or wrong into explorations of what motivates an interpretation from another reader's social location, and how interpretations can be and remain persuasive if a reader begins from a certain premise.

College level:

The Uncovering Theologies project at the university level introduces students to the complex nature of reading and interpretation. It is at university that many students grapple with the multi-valent nature of biblical texts and the vastness of interpretive traditions for the first time. Surfacing students' own latent interpretations and traditions in juxtaposed to those of their classmates greatly accelerates this discovery process. Students gain an understanding of how their world-view and traditions shape interpretation and in turn movements within traditions for good or ill. The discovery of dynamic interplay between text and reader naturally prompts questions of authorial intent in the composition of texts opening avenues for rich, engaged discussion as to what the author assumed in addressing his/her original audience and how scholars piece together a picture of the author and their audience from other extant texts of the period, mythology of surrounding cultures, the archeological record, biblical critical methodology and lens, etc.

Graduate level:

The Uncovering Theologies project, though useful for all the reasons outlined above, was designed as a tool to aid in the teaching of apocalyptic and midrashic literature. To appreciate the inventive strategies of the ancient authors engaged in proto-midrashic and midrashic interpretation of sacred texts, students must grapple with the theological constraints operating in ancient Jewish culture. The exercise of having to link or pull the biblical story through the empty frames of the novel creates a natural, experiential understanding of how the ancient authors attempting to meet pressing historical exigencies of their time both identified and exploited the narrative gaps inherent in the founding tales of Israel's sacred tradition. Having composed their own interpretation/midrashim, they were intrigued to see how their readings compared to that of ancient interpreters. The composition of the graphic novels dramatically increased the level of the students' interest and engagement in the subject.

What to do with the *Uncovering Theologies* project

The *Uncovering Theologies* project is an invitation as much to instructors as to students to think and teach creatively, to wrestle with the text and trouble interpretations. The possible uses and applications of the Uncovering Theologies project are limited only by your imagination and the time you can allot for the project in a given class. Here are some ideas to get you started:

1. **Synchronic Analysis:** Chose the work of 2-3 students and compare their interpretations at single points. Project the drawings via Power Point or a platform like Prezi allowing the entire class to see. The students are amazed at the variance of interpretation among themselves. This accomplishes several critically important things that are difficult to communicate from a lectern. Primarily, it demonstrates the inherent interpretive latitude which exists in the gaps of any given biblical text and underscores how these gaps have invited speech/commentary/interpretation for millennia; gaps which formed and are still forming community. In this they gain an understanding as to how the multiplicity of denominational interpretation of this one text (the Bible) is possible in the modern world as well as an appreciation for the difficulty of critiquing a tradition from within the tradition's own echo chamber.

2. **Diachronic Analysis:** Have students do 2 stories in the Uncovering Theologies project. Reading the stories of one student together can reveal theological themes and the base texts a student uses or draws heavily on as theological frames to make sense of the gaps in the story. Two stories offer a longer runway for students in the class to discover or recognize the texts and strategies brought to bear by the student whose work is under examination. For example, with the stories of Adam and Eve and the Akedah, one student used the frame of Job, a much later text, in both graphic novels as an explanation of divine motivation justifying the testing of the protagonists. The discovery of this triangulation allowed the student (and vicariously their classmates) to pull apart these narratives which they often do not realize are woven together in their minds.

3. **Collective Readings:** Project the work of a student locating the gap in the biblical tale it is addressing and then invite the subject's classmates to offer their interpretations. After some suggestions, then reveal the student's accompanying text and again invite class comment. After the class had their say, invite the student whose work is

being analyzed to defend/explain/verify the class' interpretation/understanding of their work. With a little guidance, this can prove a remarkably fruitful conversation. It invites other students to offer their ideas in a round-robin, come up with questions and attempt answers resulting in a high investment the conversation and deep curiosity in the text and the history of interpretation.

4. **Bring in the Rabbis and the Church Fathers:** Once students have surfaced their own interpretation of a story they find it fascinating to see how their interpretations measure up to those of ancient interpreters and other figures of history, politicians, playwrights, artists, novelist, pastors/priest ancient or modern, etc. Copy an excerpt from a Church Father or project a work of art and open the floor to discussion. With a little guidance the discussion can raise questions and considerations concerning the constraints operating on a given interpreter. This awareness on how worldviews both proscribe and constrain ideas can in turn be reflected into considerations of the student's own worldview and that of the biblical author.

5. **Peer to peer review and presentation:** Have a big class? Have the students read and review each other's graphic novels and prepare comment to share. If you have a teaching assistant or two, the class can be broken into groups for discussion and then offer representative samples of their work and discussion in a plenary session. an interpretation is right or wrong into explorations of what motivates an interpretation from another reader's social location, and how interpretations can be and remain persuasive if a reader begins from a certain premise.

The value of troubling interpretation

It is an invaluable experience for students to have their interpretations examined, prodded, and troubled. Such complication, when done with respectful curiosity, significantly increases a student's interest in the Bible and the nature of interpretation. Some interpretations are good, some inspired, some off the wall, some are dangerous. To begin to understand the Bible a student must grapple with the theological constraints operating in their own tradition and worldview. Questioning why a student holds a belief or interpretation, making them publically reason about their ideas, stretches the student in the hot seat as well as those observing the exchange as they imagine their own ideas under such examination.

Admissions:

Note – not everyone is an extrovert and/or an exhibitionist

It is rare for a student in this digital age that does not enjoy seeing their work displayed and commented on in class. Still, it is good to give an option for students who would prefer to remain anonymous or not have their novel used in the public discussion at all to be able to exempt their work. To make it clear and easy, there is a box that can be checked at the bottom of each of the student's panels indicating they prefer that segment not used in the plenary discussion.

Not a perfect experiment...
There are three nearly inescapable layers of interpretation in this version of the Uncovering Theologies project:

1. The biblical stories are pre-drawn and therefore offer interpretation in the place, posture, and expressions of the characters. Ideally the students would draw the biblical story themselves. In early experiments students were given blank frames and asked to draw the story, gap and fill the text. It proved too complicated, students spent all their time drawing the biblical scenes and missed entirely the concept of midrashic gaps in the text. Though it offers a layer of interpretation, by providing the text and drawing the scenes the students were able to focus on their interpretation and questions.

2. The gaps are provided and therefore not necessarily where the student might perceive a gap in the narrative. This is regrettable. I found through much experimentation, however, that there was no practical way around this problem that space had to be provided for the students to draw at predetermined intervals. I could not illustrate the biblical text to address the problem outlined above without also gapping the text.

3. The biblical text is the New Revised Standard Version which is a translation of the Hebrew. Languages exist in systems and while words can certainly be translated, phrases are harder, ideas, poetry, and idiom harder still as they are tied to the linguistic structures and webs of association which give them meaning. All translations are therefore, necessarily interpretations in their own right however faithful they attempt to be to the original. The use of an English translation is in service of a wider audience who can reap the benefits of the Uncovering Theologies project without first having to learn Hebrew (though, if provided the chance, they should).

ADAM AND EVE

STALLED?

USE ONE OF THESE PROMPTS

Try starting a sentence with one of the following:

Therefore...

On account of...

So that...

Because of...

For that reason...

In order to...

for context

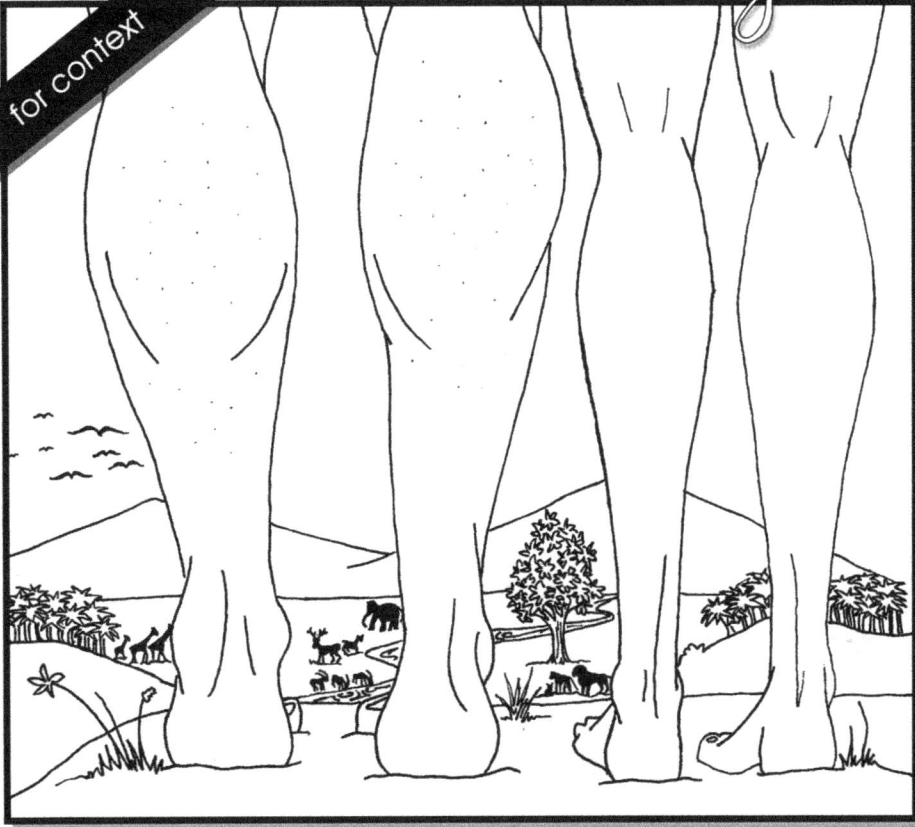

The LORD God took the man and put him in the garden of Eden to till it and keep it. And the LORD God commanded the man, "You may freely eat of every tree of the garden; but of the tree of the knowledge of good and evil you shall not eat, for in the day that you eat of it you shall die."

GENESIS 2:15-17

NEED HELP?

TROUBLE THE NARRATIVE

Think about what questions you have about this story.

There are many elements of biblical narrative that the author does not spell out. What is not explained in this story? Take a stab at clarifying that.

_____
_____
_____
_____
_____
_____
_____
_____
_____
_____
_____
_____
_____
_____
_____
_____

grade

_____
Instructor

_____
Teaching Assistant

UNCOVERING THEOLOGIES
in Genesis

Now the serpent was more crafty than any other wild animal that the LORD God had made.

GENESIS 3:1a

STUCK?

BECOME THE TEACHER

Imagine you are telling or teaching this story to someone else who has not heard it before...

How would you tell it?

What would you add?

What would a someone legitimately wonder about?

INSTRUCTOR NOTES

GENESIS 3:1a

grade

Instructor

Teaching Assistant

Name

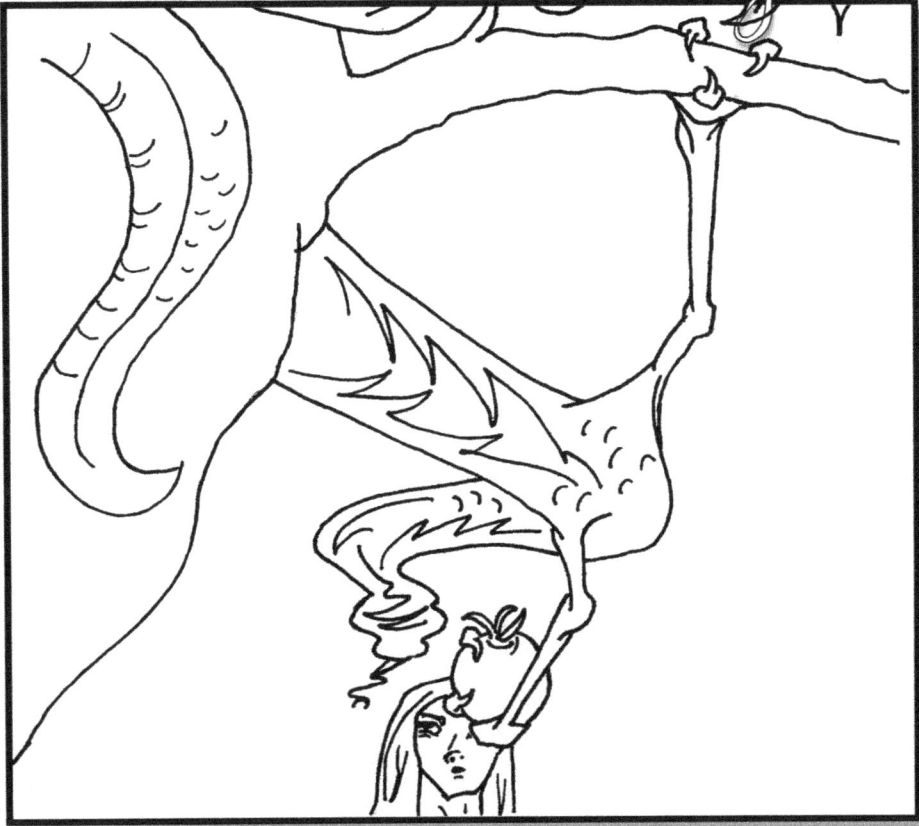

He said to the woman, "Did God say, 'You shall not eat from any tree in the garden'?" The woman said to the serpent, "We may eat of the fruit of the trees in the garden; but God said, 'You shall not eat of the fruit of the tree that is in the middle of the garden, nor shall you touch it, or you shall die.'"

GENESIS 3:1b-3

CAN'T FIND AN ANGLE

TRY THIS

Imagine you are a character in the story… what would your character need to think or need to do to justify what that character does next in the biblical text? Remember, God is a character too.

grade

_____
Instructor

_____
Teaching Assistant

UNCOVERING THEOLOGIES
in Genesis

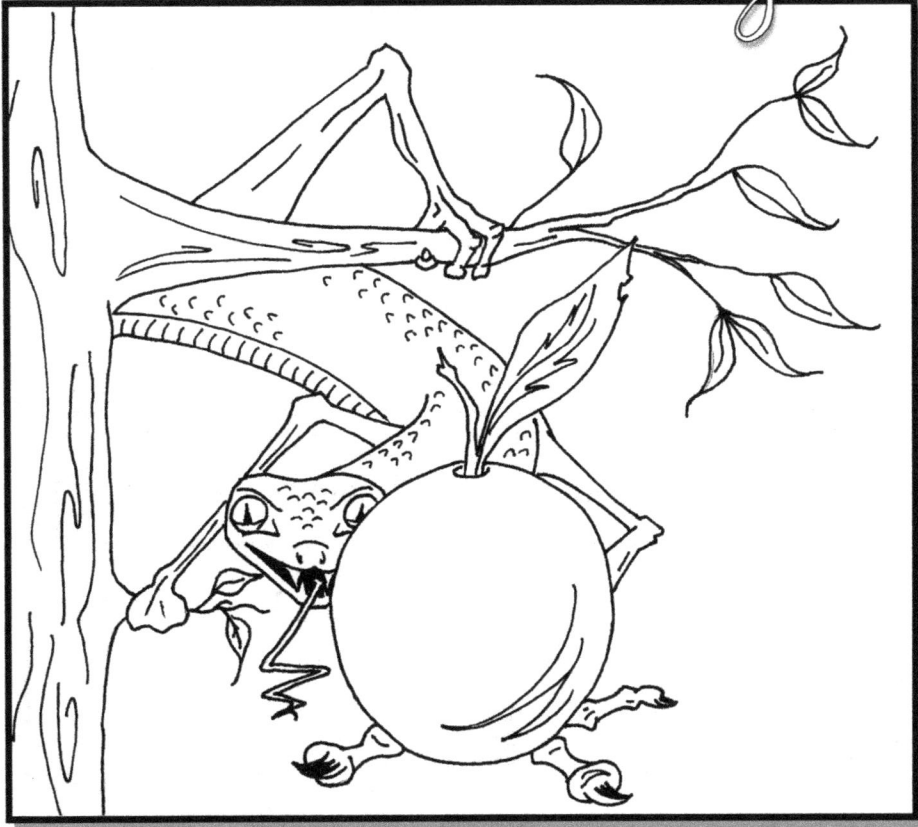

But the serpent said to the woman, "You will not die; for God knows that when you eat of it your eyes will be opened, and you will be like God, knowing good and evil."

GENESIS 3:4-5

HAVING TROUBLE?

HERE'S A TIP!

You are pulling the story through the blank frames.

What happens that makes sense of what happens in the next frame of the story?

Remember, there are no wrong answers.

Use your imagination!

grade

Instructor

Teaching Assistant

UNCOVERING THEOLOGIES in Genesis

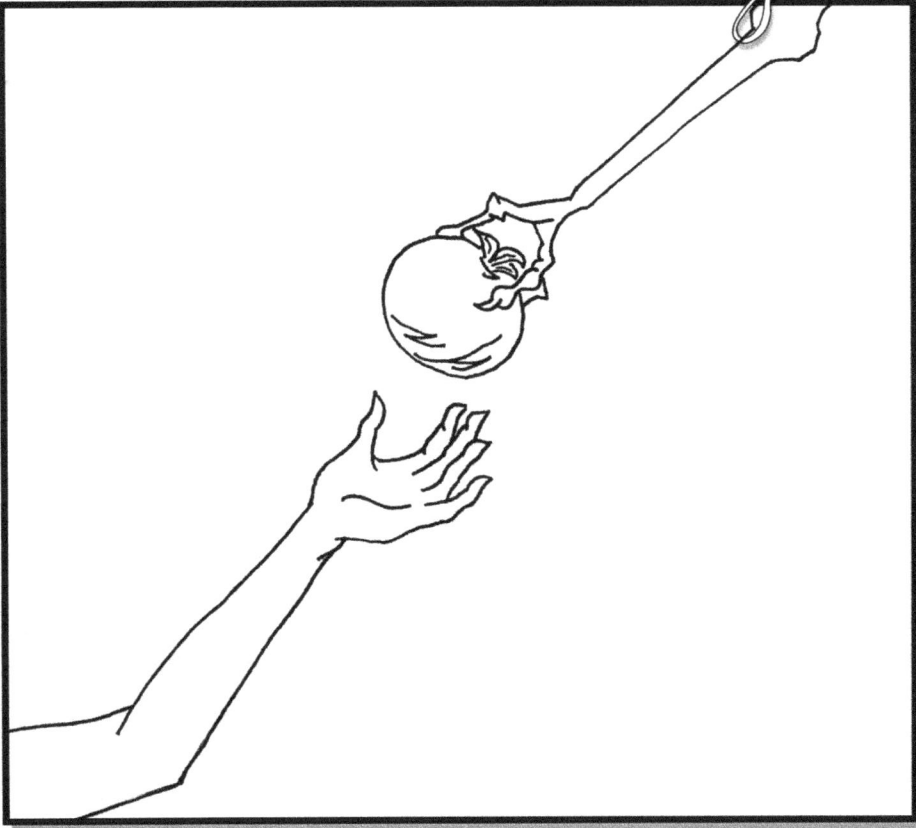

So when the woman saw that the tree was good for food, and that it was a delight to the eyes, and that the tree was to be desired to make one wise, she took of its fruit and ate; and she also gave some to her husband, who was with her, and he ate.

GENESIS 3:6

DRAWING A BLANK?

INDULGE YOUR CREATIVITY!

Do you imagine a backstory for one of the characters? An event that would explain what is happening at this point in the narrative?

grade

Instructor

Teaching Assistant

Then the eyes of both were opened, and they knew that they were naked; and they sewed fig leaves together and made loincloths for themselves.

GENESIS 3:7

STALLED?

USE ONE OF THESE PROMPTS

Try starting a sentence with one of the following:

Therefore...

On account of...

So that...

Because of...

For that reason...

In order to...

_____
_____
_____
_____
_____
_____
_____
_____
_____
_____
_____
_____
_____
_____
_____
_____
_____
_____
_____

grade

_____
Instructor

_____
Teaching Assistant

UNCOVERING THEOLOGIES
in Genesis

☐ CHECK BOX
TO OPT OUT

Name

They heard the sound of the LORD God walking in the garden at the time of the evening breeze, and the man and his wife hid themselves from the presence of the LORD God among the trees of the garden.But the LORD God called to the man, and said to him, "Where are you?" He said, "I heard the sound of you in the garden, and I was afraid, because I was naked; and I hid myself."

GENESIS 3:8-10

NEED HELP?

TROUBLE THE NARRATIVE

Think about what questions you have about this story.

There are many elements of biblical narrative that the author does not spell out. What is not explained in this story? Take a stab at clarifying that.

_____
_____
_____
_____
_____
_____
_____
_____
_____
_____
_____
_____
_____
_____

grade

_____
Instructor

_____
Teaching Assistant

UNCOVERING THEOLOGIES
in Genesis

□ CHECK BOX
TO OPT OUT

He said, "Who told you that you were naked? Have you eaten from the tree of which I commanded you not to eat? "The man said, "The woman whom you gave to be with me, she gave me fruit from the tree, and I ate."

GENESIS 3:11-12

STUCK?

BECOME THE TEACHER

Imagine you are telling or teaching this story to someone else who has not heard it before...

How would you tell it?

What would you add?

What would a someone legitimately wonder about?

_____
_____
_____
_____
_____
_____
_____
_____
_____
_____
_____
_____
_____
_____

grade

_____
Instructor

_____
Teaching Assistant

UNCOVERING THEOLOGIES
in Genesis

Then the LORD God said to the woman, "What is this that you have done?" The woman said, "The serpent tricked me, and I ate."

GENESIS 3:13

CAN'T FIND AN ANGLE

TRY THIS

Imagine you are a character in the story… what would your character need to think or need to do to justify what that character does next in the biblical text? Remember, God is a character too.

grade

Instructor

Teaching Assistant

UNCOVERING THEOLOGIES in Genesis

☐ CHECK BOX
TO OPT OUT

The LORD God said to the serpent, "Because you have done this, cursed are you among all animals and among all wild creatures; upon your belly you shall go, and dust you shall eat all the days of your life. I will put enmity between you and the woman, and between your offspring and hers; he will strike your head, and you will strike his heel."

GENESIS 3:14-15

HAVING TROUBLE?

HERE'S A TIP!

You are pulling the story through the blank frames.

What happens that makes sense of what happens in the next frame of the story?

Remember, there are no wrong answers.

Use your imagination!

grade

Instructor

Teaching Assistant

Name

To the woman he said, "I will greatly increase your pangs in childbearing; in pain you shall bring forth children, yet your desire shall be for your husband, and he shall rule over you."

GENESIS 3:16

23

DRAWING A BLANK?

INDULGE YOUR CREATIVITY!

Do you imagine a backstory for one of the characters? An event that would explain what is happening at this point in the narrative?

_____
_____
_____
_____
_____
_____
_____
_____
_____
_____
_____
_____
_____
_____
_____

grade

_____
Instructor

_____
Teaching Assistant

UNCOVERING THEOLOGIES
in Genesis

CHECK BOX
TO OPT OUT

And to the man he said, "Because you have listened to the voice of your wife, and have eaten of the tree about which I commanded you, 'You shall not eat of it,' cursed is the ground because of you; in toil you shall eat of it all the days of your life; thorns and thistles it shall bring forth for you; and you shall eat the plants of the field. By the sweat of your face you shall eat bread until you return to the ground, for out of it you were taken; you are dust, and to dust you shall return."

GENESIS 3:17-19

STALLED?

USE ONE OF THESE PROMPTS

Try starting a sentence with one of the following:

Therefore...

On account of...

So that...

Because of...

For that reason...

In order to...

INSTRUCTOR NOTES
GENESIS 3:17-19

_____

_____

_____

_____

_____

_____

_____

_____

_____

_____

_____

_____

_____

_____

_____

_____

_____

_____

_____

_____

grade

_____
Instructor

_____
Teaching Assistant

UNCOVERING THEOLOGIES
in Genesis

☐ CHECK BOX
TO OPT OUT

The man named his wife Eve, because she was the mother of all living.

GENESIS 3:20

NEED HELP?

TROUBLE THE NARRATIVE

Think about what questions you have about this story.

There are many elements of biblical narrative that the author does not spell out. What is not explained in this story? Take a stab at clarifying that.

GENESIS 3:20

grade

Instructor

Teaching Assistant

Name

And the LORD God made garments of skins for the man and for his wife, and clothed them.

GENESIS 3:21

29

STUCK?

BECOME THE TEACHER

Imagine you are telling or teaching this story to someone else who has not heard it before...

How would you tell it?

What would you add?

What would a someone legitimately wonder about?

_____
_____
_____
_____
_____
_____
_____
_____
_____
_____
_____
_____
_____
_____
_____
_____
_____

grade

_____
Instructor

_____
Teaching Assistant

UNCOVERING THEOLOGIES in Genesis

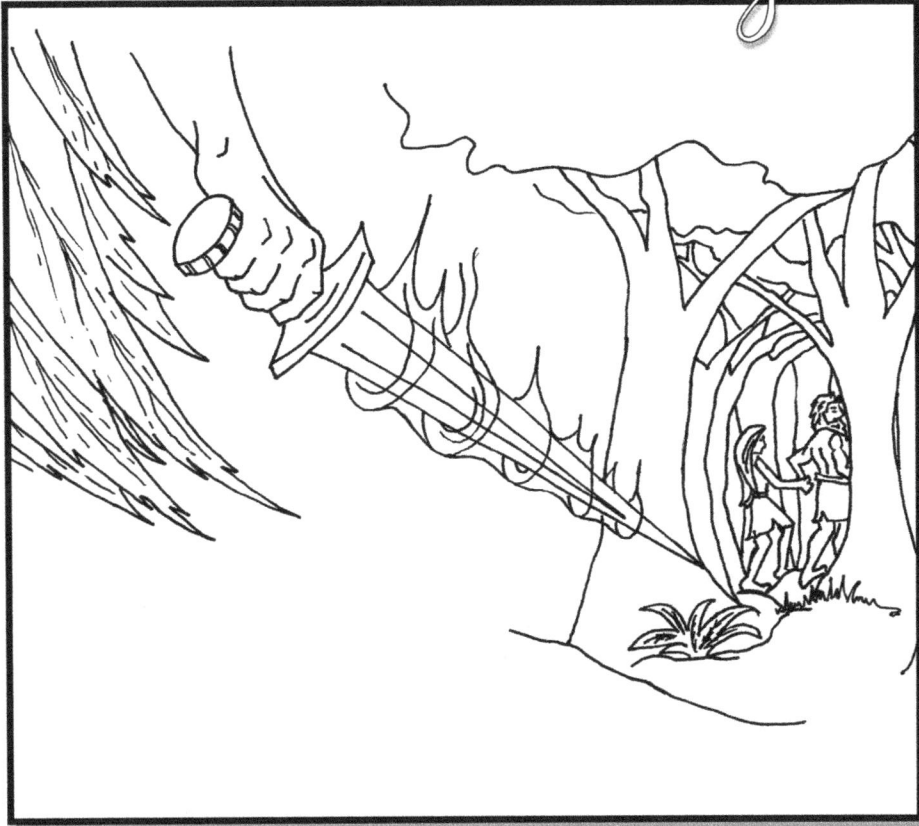

Then the LORD God said, "See, the man has become like one of us, knowing good and evil; and now, he might reach out his hand and take also from the tree of life, and eat, and live forever" – therefore the LORD God sent him forth from the garden of Eden, to till the ground from which he was taken. He drove out the man; and at the east of the garden of Eden he placed the cherubim, and a sword flaming and turning to guard the way to the tree of life.

GENESIS 3:22-24

-fin-

_____
_____
_____
_____
_____
_____
_____
_____
_____
_____
_____
_____
_____

grade

_____
Instructor

_____
Teaching Assistant

CAIN AND ABEL

CAN'T FIND AN ANGLE

TRY THIS

Imagine you are a character in the story… what would your character need to think or need to do to justify what that character does next in the biblical text? Remember, God is a character too.

UNCOVERING THEOLOGIES
in Genesis

Now the man knew his wife Eve, and she conceived and bore Cain, saying, "I have produced a man with the help of the LORD."Next she bore his brother Abel.

GENESIS 4:1-2a

HAVING TROUBLE?

HERE'S A TIP!

You are pulling the story through the blank frames.

What happens that makes sense of what happens in the next frame of the story?

Remember, there are no wrong answers.

Use your imagination!

INSTRUCTOR NOTES

GENESIS 4:1-2a

_____

_____

_____

_____

_____

_____

_____

_____

_____

_____

_____

_____

_____

_____

_____

_____

grade

_____
Instructor

_____
Teaching Assistant

Now Abel was a keeper of sheep,

GENESIS 4:2b

DRAWING A BLANK?

INDULGE YOUR CREATIVITY!

Do you imagine a backstory for one of the characters? An event that would explain what is happening at this point in the narrative?

grade

_____ Instructor

_____ Teaching Assistant

Name

and Cain a tiller of the ground.

GENESIS 4:2c

STALLED?

USE ONE OF THESE PROMPTS

Try starting a sentence with one of the following:

- Therefore...
- On account of...
- So that...
- Because of...
- For that reason...
- In order to...

grade

Instructor

Teaching Assistant

Name

In the course of time Cain brought to the LORD an offering of the fruit of the ground, and Abel for his part brought of the firstlings of his flock, their fat portions.

GENESIS 4:3-4a

NEED HELP?

TROUBLE THE NARRATIVE

Think about what questions you have about this story.

There are many elements of biblical narrative that the author does not spell out. What is not explained in this story? Take a stab at clarifying that.

_____
_____
_____
_____
_____
_____
_____
_____
_____
_____
_____
_____
_____
_____
_____
_____
_____

grade

_____
Instructor

_____
Teaching Assistant

UNCOVERING THEOLOGIES
in Genesis

☐ CHECK BOX
TO OPT OUT

And the LORD had regard for Abel and his offering, but for Cain and his offering he had no regard.

GENESIS 4:4b-5a

STUCK?

BECOME THE TEACHER

Imagine you are telling or teaching this story to someone else who has not heard it before...

How would you tell it?

What would you add?

What would a someone legitimately wonder about?

GENESIS 4:4b-5a

_____
_____
_____
_____
_____
_____
_____
_____
_____
_____
_____
_____
_____
_____

grade

_____
Instructor

_____
Teaching Assistant

UNCOVERING THEOLOGIES
in Genesis

CHECK BOX TO OPT OUT

So Cain was very angry, and his countenance fell. The LORD said to Cain, "Why are you angry, and why has your countenance fallen? If you do well, will you not be accepted? And if you do not do well, sin is lurking at the door; its desire is for you, but you must master it."

GENESIS 4:5b-7

CAN'T FIND AN ANGLE

TRY THIS

Imagine you are a character in the story… what would your character need to think or need to do to justify what that character does next in the biblical text? Remember, God is a character too.

_____
_____
_____
_____
_____
_____
_____
_____
_____
_____
_____
_____
_____
_____
_____
_____

grade

_____
Instructor

_____
Teaching Assistant

Cain said to his brother Abel, "Let us go out to the field."

GENESIS 4:8a

HAVING TROUBLE?

HERE'S A TIP!

You are pulling the story through the blank frames.

What happens that makes sense of what happens in the next frame of the story?

Remember, there are no wrong answers.

Use your imagination!

grade

Instructor

Teaching Assistant

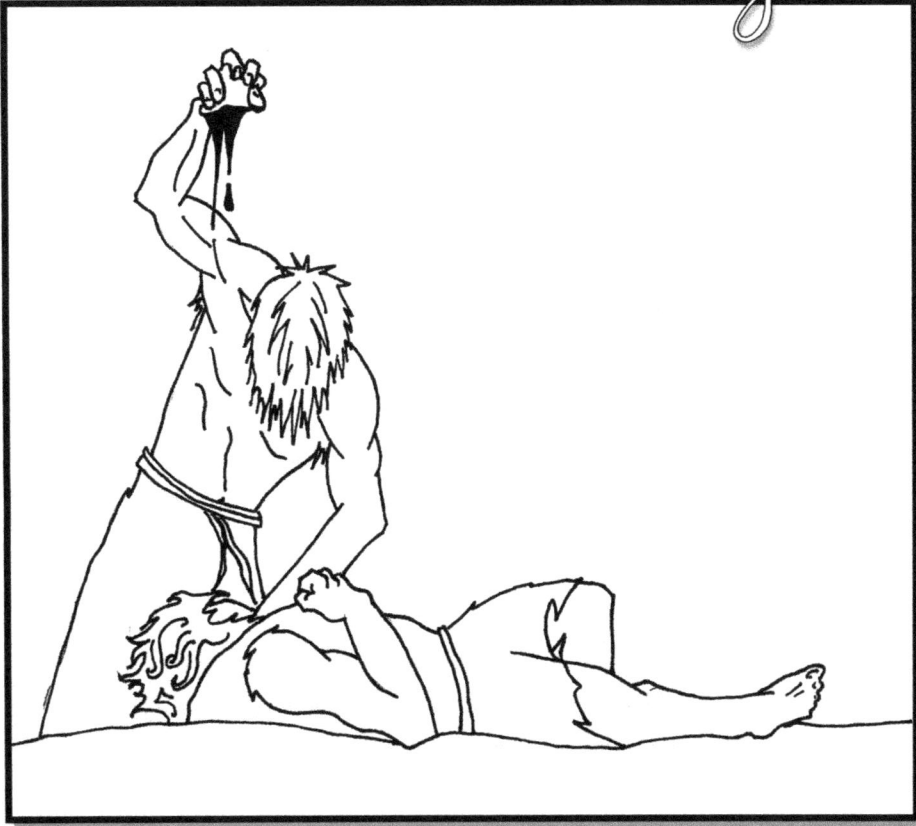

And when they were in the field, Cain rose up against his
brother Abel, and killed him.

GENESIS 4:8b

DRAWING A BLANK?

INDULGE YOUR CREATIVITY!

Do you imagine a backstory for one of the characters? An event that would explain what is happening at this point in the narrative?

grade

Instructor

Teaching Assistant

UNCOVERING THEOLOGIES
in Genesis

Then the LORD said to Cain, "Where is your brother Abel?"
He said, "I do not know; am I my brother's keeper?"

GENESIS 4:9

STALLED?

USE ONE OF THESE PROMPTS

Try starting a sentence with one of the following:

- Therefore...
- On account of...
- So that...
- Because of...
- For that reason...
- In order to...

grade

Instructor

Teaching Assistant

UNCOVERING THEOLOGIES
in Genesis

And the LORD said, "What have you done? Listen; your brother's blood is crying out to me from the ground! And now you are cursed from the ground, which has opened its mouth to receive your brother's blood from your hand. When you till the ground, it will no longer yield to you its strength; you will be a fugitive and a wanderer on the earth."

GENESIS 4:10-12

NEED HELP?

TROUBLE THE NARRATIVE

Think about what questions you have about this story.

There are many elements of biblical narrative that the author does not spell out. What is not explained in this story? Take a stab at clarifying that.

_____
_____
_____
_____
_____
_____
_____
_____
_____
_____
_____
_____
_____
_____
_____
_____

grade

_____
Instructor

_____
Teaching Assistant

Cain said to the LORD, "My punishment is greater than I can bear! Today you have driven me away from the soil, and I shall be hidden from your face; I shall be a fugitive and a wanderer on the earth, and anyone who meets me may kill me."

GENESIS 4:13-14

STUCK?

BECOME THE TEACHER

Imagine you are telling or teaching this story to someone else who has not heard it before...

How would you tell it?

What would you add?

What would a someone legitimately wonder about?

INSTRUCTOR NOTES

GENESIS 4:13-14

_____
_____
_____
_____
_____
_____
_____
_____
_____
_____
_____
_____
_____
_____

grade

Instructor

Teaching Assistant

Then the LORD said to him, "Not so! Whoever kills Cain will suffer a sevenfold vengeance." And the LORD put a mark on Cain, so that no one who came upon him would kill him.

GENESIS 4:15

CAN'T FIND AN ANGLE

TRY THIS

Imagine you are a character in the story… what would your character need to think or need to do to justify what that character does next in the biblical text? Remember, God is a character too.

grade

_____
Instructor

_____
Teaching Assistant

UNCOVERING THEOLOGIES in Genesis

Name

Then Cain went away from the presence of the LORD, and settled in the land of Nod, east of Eden.

GENESIS 4:16

INSTRUCTOR NOTES
GENESIS 4:16

-fin-

_____

_____

_____

_____

_____

_____

_____

_____

_____

_____

_____

_____

_____

grade

_____
Instructor

_____
Teaching Assistant

SACRIFICE OF ISAAC

HAVING TROUBLE?

HERE'S A TIP!

You are pulling the story through the blank frames.

What happens that makes sense of what happens in the next frame of the story?

Remember, there are no wrong answers.

Use your imagination!

UNCOVERING THEOLOGIES
in Genesis

After these things God tested Abraham. He said to him, "Abraham!" And he said, "Here I am. "He said, "Take your son, your only son Isaac, whom you love, and go to the land of Moriah, and offer him there as a burnt offering on one of the mountains that I shall show you."

GENESIS 22:1-2

DRAWING A BLANK?

INDULGE YOUR CREATIVITY!

Do you imagine a backstory for one of the characters? An event that would explain what is happening at this point in the narrative?

grade

Instructor

Teaching Assistant

So Abraham rose early in the morning

GENESIS 22:3a

STALLED?

USE ONE OF THESE PROMPTS

Try starting a sentence with one of the following:

- Therefore...
- On account of...
- So that...
- Because of...
- For that reason...
- In order to...

grade

Instructor

Teaching Assistant

UNCOVERING THEOLOGIES
in Genesis

Name

saddled his donkey, and took two of his young men with him, and his son Isaac; he cut the wood for the burnt offering,

GENESIS 22:3b

NEED HELP?

TROUBLE THE NARRATIVE

Think about what questions you have about this story.

There are many elements of biblical narrative that the author does not spell out. What is not explained in this story? Take a stab at clarifying that.

_____
_____
_____
_____
_____
_____
_____
_____
_____
_____
_____
_____
_____
_____
_____

grade

Instructor

Teaching Assistant

and set out and went to the place in the distance that God had shown him. On the third day Abraham looked up and saw the place far away.

GENESIS 22:3c-4

STUCK?

BECOME THE TEACHER

Imagine you are telling or teaching this story to someone else who has not heard it before...

How would you tell it?

What would you add?

What would a someone legitimately wonder about?

grade

Instructor

Teaching Assistant

UNCOVERING THEOLOGIES
in Genesis

Then Abraham said to his young men, "Stay here with the donkey; the boy and I will go over there; we will worship, and then we will come back to you."

GENESIS 22:5

CAN'T FIND AN ANGLE

TRY THIS

Imagine you are a character in the story... what would your character need to think or need to do to justify what that character does next in the biblical text? Remember, God is a character too.

grade

_____ Instructor

_____ Teaching Assistant

UNCOVERING THEOLOGIES
in Genesis

CHECK BOX
TO OPT OUT

Abraham took the wood of the burnt offering and laid it on his son Isaac, and he himself carried the fire and the knife. So the two of them walked on together. Isaac said to his father Abraham, "Father!" And he said, "Here I am, my son." He said, "The fire and the wood are here, but where is the lamb for a burnt offering?" Abraham said, "God himself will provide the lamb for a burnt offering, my son." So the two of them walked on together.

GENESIS 22:6-8

HAVING TROUBLE?

HERE'S A TIP!

You are pulling the story through the blank frames.

What happens that makes sense of what happens in the next frame of the story?

Remember, there are no wrong answers.

Use your imagination!

INSTRUCTOR NOTES

GENESIS 22:6-8

grade

Instructor

Teaching Assistant

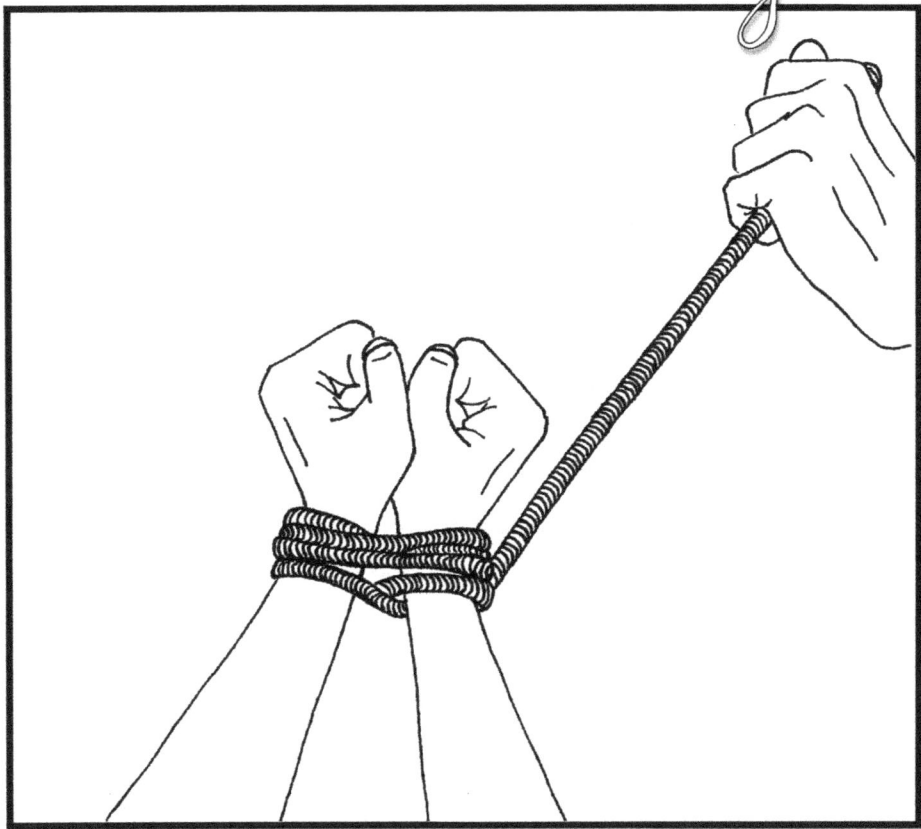

When they came to the place that God had shown him, Abraham built an altar there and laid the wood in order. He bound his son Isaac, and laid him on the altar, on top of the wood.

GENESIS 22:9

DRAWING A BLANK?

INDULGE YOUR CREATIVITY!

Do you imagine a backstory for one of the characters? An event that would explain what is happening at this point in the narrative?

grade

Instructor

Teaching Assistant

Then Abraham reached out his hand and took the knife to kill his son.

GENESIS 22:10

STALLED?

USE ONE OF THESE PROMPTS

Try starting a sentence with one of the following:

Therefore...

On account of...

So that...

Because of...

For that reason...

In order to...

INSTRUCTOR NOTES

GENESIS 22:10

_____
_____
_____
_____
_____
_____
_____
_____
_____
_____
_____
_____
_____
_____

grade

_____
Instructor

_____
Teaching Assistant

UNCOVERING THEOLOGIES
in Genesis

Name

But the angel of the LORD called to him from heaven, and said, "Abraham, Abraham!" And he said, "Here I am. "He said, "Do not lay your hand on the boy or do anything to him; for now I know that you fear God, since you have not withheld your son, your only son, from me."

GENESIS 22:11-12

NEED HELP?

TROUBLE THE NARRATIVE

Think about what questions you have about this story.

There are many elements of biblical narrative that the author does not spell out. What is not explained in this story? Take a stab at clarifying that.

grade

Instructor

Teaching Assistant

UNCOVERING THEOLOGIES
in Genesis

Name _____

And Abraham looked up and saw a ram, caught in a thicket by its horns. Abraham went and took the ram and offered it up as a burnt offering instead of his son.

GENESIS 22:13

STUCK?

BECOME THE TEACHER

Imagine you are telling or teaching this story to someone else who has not heard it before...

How would you tell it?

What would you add?

What would a someone legitimately wonder about?

_____
_____
_____
_____
_____
_____
_____
_____
_____
_____
_____
_____
_____
_____
_____
_____

grade

_____
Instructor

_____
Teaching Assistant

UNCOVERING THEOLOGIES
in Genesis

So Abraham called that place "The LORD will provide"; as it is said to this day, "On the mount of the LORD it shall be provided."

GENESIS 22:14

CAN'T FIND AN ANGLE

TRY THIS

Imagine you are a character in the story… what would your character need to think or need to do to justify what that character does next in the biblical text? Remember, God is a character too.

grade

_____ Instructor

_____ Teaching Assistant

Name

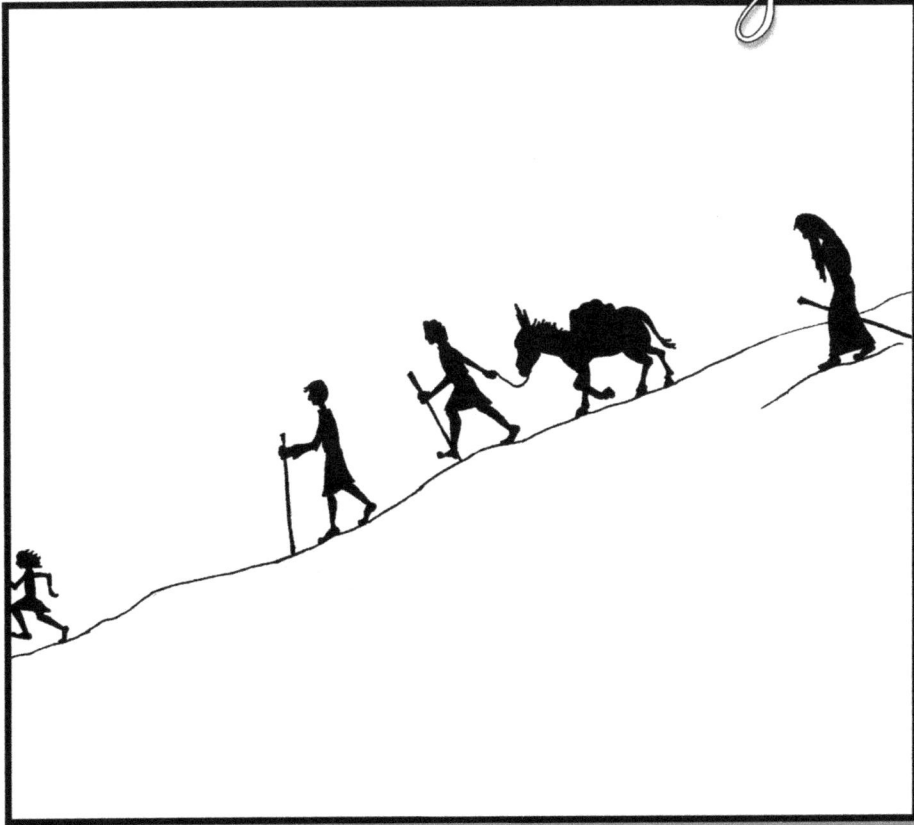

The angel of the LORD called to Abraham a second time from heaven, and said, "By myself I have sworn, says the LORD: Because you have done this, and have not withheld your son, your only son, I will indeed bless you, and I will make your offspring as numerous as the stars of heaven and as the sand that is on the seashore. And your offspring shall possess the gate of their enemies, and by your offspring shall all the nations of the earth gain blessing for themselves, because you have obeyed my voice. "So Abraham returned to his young men, and they arose and went together to Beer-sheba; and Abraham lived at Beer-sheba.

GENESIS 22:15-19

INSTRUCTOR NOTES
GENESIS 22:15-19

Instructor

Teaching Assistant

Grade

-*Jim*-